BRITAIN IN OLD PH

G000280125

TAUNTON REMEMBERED

NICK CHIPCHASE

SUTTON PUBLISHING

Sutton Publishing Limited
Phoenix Mill · Thrupp · Stroud
Gloucestershire · GL5 2BU

First published 2007

Copyright © Nick Chipchase, 2007

Title page photograph: Times gone by, *c.* 1900.
A farmer walks his cow through the village
at Blagdon Hill.

British Library Cataloguing in Publication Data
A catalogue record for this book is available from the
British Library.

ISBN 978-07509-4676-6

Typeset in 10.5/13.5 Photina.
Typesetting and origination by
Sutton Publishing Limited.
Printed and bound in England.

Taunton from the air, *c.* 1936. The new County Hall is shining bright in the sunshine and the rest of the
Crescent Fields have still to be built on. At the top, to the north-east, there are still green fields, now
swallowed up by the expansion of the town. (*Aerofilms*)

CONTENTS

The County Museum, Great Hall, *c.* 1904. These natural history exhibits were laid out by
Somerset and Natural History Society (SANHS) shortly after the museum's reopening
in 1902. *(Abraham)*

These nine cartes de visites show Taunton ladies and girls from the 1850s to the 1890s. All were taken in the studios of professional photographers in the town.

INTRODUCTION

This is my fifth book of local images for Sutton Publishing leaving me little new to say about the historical aspects of Taunton and its environs. It does, however, give me the opportunity to look at the development of photography in the area and look ahead to the massive changes we expect to see in the next twenty-five years.

Social history is all about the process of change and the styles and trends that come and go. Sometimes the patterns repeat themselves. Without the photographers who recorded these changes over the last 150 years we would not be able to see how life has altered so considerably. As we travel further into the twenty-first century we can be sure that social conditions will continue to change even faster than before.

The photographs in my own collection have been collected over a space of thirty years. The majority date from between 1902 and 1914, the so called 'golden age' of postcard publication when countless cards were produced and sent all over the

West Monkton post office, *c.* 1906. Sarah Ellen Gardener was postmistress at this time. This area may be swallowed up by the continued expansion of Taunton.

world. It is interesting to note the origin of these postcards, for without them little would survive from this era. Few ordinary folk owned a camera and home negatives gave poor results. From records I have kept, the postcards from my area of interest originated from eighty-eight national professional photographers, fourteen local professional photographers and fifty-three amateur local photographers.

The views of the big national photographers do tend to be formulaic. The photographers often came early to get the best light and took views of a largely deserted town showing little in the way of social history. They provide a good record of the main streets and buildings but little else. The local photographers had more feel for the place, adopting different angles of view and showing local events and businesses. No subject seemed beyond their interest and some scenes would only have sold to a very limited market. A view of the gas works is one example.

Henry Montague Cooper was the most prolific local professional with five studios operating in the west country. Only two of Cooper's photographs feature in this book as I will be dedicating an entire book to his life and work.

The amateurs in the area included bakers, newsagents, shopkeepers and a vicar. The known work of some of these amateurs accounts for less than a dozen images.

William Stone, a young solicitor's clerk living with his aunt, produced a few early views. It is obvious he was still experimenting but by 1904 he was proudly calling himself William Stone, Photographer. The vicar of Fivehead produced an early set depicting village life to raise funds for the church tower restoration. Some of the existing copies are now badly faded. Some exemplary work with long-lasting developing techniques was done by Brass and Mitchell, both bakers at Creech St Michael. In Taunton itself good photographic work was also produced by newsagent John Brice, who had a particular interest in back streets not photographed by anybody else.

We can never know the extent of the work done by these people as so much has been lost over the years. Many Frith negatives remain to provide early images of main streets and churches. Sadly Montague Cooper's stock was taken to the tip when his business closed. For the contemporary collector the heyday has passed. Most of the intact albums of postcards have been recovered and broken up for sale. Yet the blossoming of the internet means there is now a global market for anything and individual treasures still come to light.

The internet now plays a huge part in research and promotion of hobbies. We can look at an early photograph of a place and find out who lived there. We can even identify people in the picture. The arrival of the 1901 Census online has helped social historians and genealogists alike. The two little old ladies at Isle Abbots on page 119 are no longer strangers in a landscape. They can be identified and are now part of the story, lost for decades. Anna and Ellen Patten were born in the village in the 1830s and probably never left it, being content not to marry but to run the local post office and shop until they were too old to continue. It is also possible to look at an entire street. I was able to confirm that the Great Western Railway was the main employer in the Thomas Street area, for example. Living conditions were good with an average of four people per household, and jobs were diverse and plentiful. Working-class people in Taunton in 1901 were certainly not

The asylum at Cotford. *c.* 1910. The buildings and part of the surrounding area now form the new village of Cotford St Luke. *(E.E. Cox)*

short of employment, with the railways, shirt and collar factories, breweries and agricultural trades doing well.

I have tried to focus on areas which are still topical and where life has changed greatly. Several early post offices are shown highlighting the continuing argument about closures. These closures seem inevitable. A hundred years ago a village of 200 people could support a sub-post office. This is no longer possible. Since 1997 a quarter of existing post offices have closed reducing the number to 14,000. Another 2,500 closures have recently been announced. The decline in public houses has mirrored that of the post offices. Taunton had around ninety pubs a hundred years ago, one for every 230 of the town's inhabitants. That ratio has now changed dramatically with under forty pubs catering for 60,000 townsfolk. Closures in Taunton since 1970 include the Oak and Acorn, the Plough, the Foresters, the Telegraph, the Frieze Hill, the Full Moon, the Harp, the Masons Arms, and the Turks Head. Others have had makeovers and new names, including the Cherry Grove (the Grove), the Dolphin (Flying Horse), Royal Mail (the Cricketers), and the Cottage at Monkton Heathfield (Merry Monk).

The pace of change in Taunton has not only been constant but is now accelerating; far fewer photographers will be around to record the process. There has been the creation of a new village at Cotford St Luke and massive housing developments around the town. Taunton's impending status as a Principal Urban Area is worrying many. Certainly the property price rise has resulted in a return to town living with residential developments replacing many industrial sites. In a much more acceptable way this mirrors the interwar courts of Taunton. Their demolition and clearance heralded the outward urban expansion of the town. Big garages came into the town tearing great holes in the linear development of small shops. Three are now gone to be replaced by developments like the residential Belvedere Gardens, itself adjoining Laverock House on the site of the old Classic Cinema. The cycle has come full circle.

Outlying villages have not remained untouched. Some like Wrantage, Bradford on Tone, Thornfalcon, and Staple Fitzpaine are no larger than they were twenty years ago. Others have rocketed in population: Cheddon Fitzpaine from 420 to 1,300, West Monkton from 1,850 to 2,420 and Comeytrowe from 4,940 to 5,710 inhabitants. The town itself has almost trebled its population in 100 years.

Now Taunton is at the dawn of its greatest change in history. No more will it be a market town but, as the 'Vision for Taunton' declares, 'The Taunton of 2025 will be an exemplar of a twenty-first century town'. It will no longer be a county town but a 'Regional Centre', part of the local government district of Taunton Deane stretching from the Tone to the county border, a region of 45,000 dwellings and 4,500 businesses with a population of well over 100,000. In the town itself will come 47 hectares of redevelopment, 2,200 new houses and apartments, 80,000sq m of new employment spaces, and 50,000sq m of new retail and leisure facilities. Added to this will be a new library, a new hotel, a new bus station, an extended and refurbished cricket ground, a new theatre and over 2km of enhanced town centre riverfront. There will also be two new road links crossing the river. Indeed the Taunton of 2025 will be very different from how it is now.

The factors we cannot predict will also influence change. Will we see a repeat of the devastating floods of the 1880s, 1929 and 1960? Will the massive change we are experiencing in demographics play a part? Can local industries be maintained? Taunton is still the preferred home for the Hydrographic Office (1,000 staff), the Charity Commission (220 staff) and Western Provident Association (300 staff). The town's future prosperity will depend on big players like these.

My five books to date have been a joy to compile. My collection has given me a grandstand view of the changes in Taunton throughout the twentieth century. I hope people will find this new book as interesting as I have found its compilation. Taunton has changed so much and will continue to do so.

Nick Chipchase, 2007

1

Street Scenes

The Parade, *c.* 1905. The Parade forms the centre of Taunton. In the background is the Kinglake Memorial, erected in 1867 and demolished in 1934. Many Tauntonians expected the cross to be re-erected but only the top remained – in a garden at Kingston St Mary for many years.

East Street, *c.* 1906. On the right is the London Hotel bought by Ernest Claridge in 1901; he ran it until 1913. Mr Claridge introduced his famous horse bus in 1903.

East Reach, *c.* 1906. Sibley and Thorne's Dress, Mantle and Millinery Warehouse, extreme left, in later years became the site for Pearsall's silk factory. Beyond this is George Paul's the pawnbroker at 1 East Reach. The single-decker tram climbs East Reach hill, one of the steepest sections of the system. Slightly different tramway standards are being used here than in the above view, being placed on both sides of the street.

Fore Street, c. 1929. This unusual view was taken from inside the Market House arcades, which were removed in 1930. On the right is Gibson and Harrison's, hairdressers at 6 Fore Street. This became the headquarters for St John Ambulance in the 1950s.

Fore Street and Burmah Cross, c. 1904. The end of the Market House arcade is in view. The Burmah Cross was erected in 1889 but removed to its current position in recent years to form a focal point for the traffic roundabout on the Parade. To the right is the ornate building of the Somerset County Club, which opened in 1880.

Fore Street, *c.* 1914. View towards the Market House. On the right is Clements and Brown, general and family drapers, costumiers and milliners. For a while the company had a smaller store at 15 Bridge Street. The Fore Street store was extended in 1907. On the left is Marshalsea's Automobile Association listed motor garage, now the Abbey building society. The company moved the garage to Wellington Road in about 1920. The man in the middle of the road is standing in the centre of one of the tramway's passing loops.

Fore Street, *c.* 1904. This view shows the Burmese Memorial (erected 1889) in its original location before it was moved to the Parade. The large building, extreme left, is the County Club. Behind the memorial is F.W. Baker's music warehouse followed by Barnicott and Pearce, printers, then Holt's the tobacconists. The Home and Colonial Stores and Clements and Brown are also seen in the photograph above.

Fore Street, *c.* 1903. This photograph was taken by Mr W.H. Stone of Flook Villa who produced a range of amateur postcards in 1903 and 1904. To the right on the corner of Hammett Street is Fox, Fowler and Co.'s fine bank building, now demolished. The tram is double-decker car no. 3 viewed from the rear. The 'fishing rod' arm collected the current to power the electric motor. Car no. 3 was built by Brush in 1901 and was part of a fleet of six double-deckers.

Corporation Street, *c.* 1936. The street was constructed in 1893/4 and originally held the town's educational establishments – the free library, the school of art and the technological institute, the tower of which can be seen in the centre. The Gaumont Cinema was built in 1932 when a new road called Castle Way was cut through to provide access to Tower Street. Somerset Motors' car showrooms can be seen on the left.

Castle Bow then open to two-way traffic, *c.* 1960. The lorry on the left is being used by a vendor selling fruit and vegetables. Burtons bought the corner section of the Castle Hotel from Harrisons Hotels Ltd and their foundation stone, laid in 1929, can still be seen at the road level. Although on the site of the castle east gate, none of the portcullis and archway is original.

High Street, *c.* 1902. To the left is the sign of the Full Moon Inn. Now pedestrianised, the long wide street with its rows of plane trees was a major thoroughfare in Victorian times.

High Street, *c.* 1950. The building on the left with the large sign is the Three Mariners snack bar. Next is Arnold and Hancock's Green Dragon Inn. The greater part of this area of the street is now estate agents and mortgage lenders. Hatchers had the centre building built in 1894 but it is now a bar.

Fore Street looking east, 1935. The Devon and Somerset Stores, extreme right, stands on the corner of High Street. The building was demolished in the 1960s.

Fore Street looking north, 1935. Notice the roundabout servicing Corporation Street, High Street and Fore Street. There are four bus stands adjacent to the Parade for services to the Holway area, Chard, Honiton, Sidmouth, Glastonbury, Seaton, Burnham and Yeovil.

The Parade from Corporation Street, 1935. The 180ft tower of St Mary's Church dominates the skyline. The roundabout system was introduced after the demolition of the Market House arcades in 1930.

Mixed transport on the Parade, c. 1906. This view includes a Great Western Railway delivery cart, a motor car, an electric tram, a carriage and hansom cabs. An electric arc lamp stands in front of the Kinglake memorial. Taunton has had permanent electric street lighting since 1886.

The Parade and Market House, c. 1905. The old Market House on the south side of the Parade together with other buildings was demolished by the newly formed Market Trustees in 1768. The new Market House was completed in 1772. The trustees added a new market building (later known as the Victorian Rooms) in 1821. From 1934 this building became the town hall; it was demolished in the mid-1960s. A Corn Exchange was built adjacent to Castle Bow in 1853 and was removed in 1937 to build new showrooms for the Electricity Board.

Hammet Street and St Mary's, *c.* 1904. On the left is Fox, Fowler and Co.'s fine bank building. The majority of the buildings on the left housed the offices of solicitors. The shop immediately to the right is Kelsey and Tyler, athletic outfitters, followed by three other shops and then more offices. The street was built in 1788 to provide this fine view of St Mary's tower. The tower was completely demolished and then rebuilt in the 1860s.

North Street, *c.* 1913. On the left is Hanbury and Cotching's Half Moon Hotel followed by the post office. This opened on 19 March 1911 having been built by Pollard of Bridgwater on the site of the old Spread Eagle Inn. The clock was added by public subscription two months later.

North Street, *c.* 1912. On the right is Cousins the florist's delivery cart which they used up to the 1920s. The car registration Y302 was first issued to a Rolls-Royce on 29 December 1904 but subsequently transferred to another vehicle. William Potter at 39 North Street, in business before 1900, was a hairdresser, gentleman's hosier, hatter, glover and shirt maker.

The Bridge, *c.* 1914. This modern bridge replaced the old stone structure in 1894. It is actually somewhat shorter now as the Dellers building was added to Bridge House, near the centre of the photograph. Belben Brothers on the right originally started as a 6½d Bazaar at 3 Bridge Street before expanding into a cash furnishers.

Grays Road, *c.* 1905. The postcard was sent to May Howell who had emigrated to Canada from Taunton. Interestingly the sender says 'you can get any street in Taunton on a postcard'. This view is by Taunton photographer Henry Montague Cooper who sold thousands of postcards between 1902 and 1914.

Opposite, top: Shops in Bridge Street, *c.* 1890. Ruth Trump stands in the doorway of no. 15a. She was a dealer in tea and tobacco. The 1901 Census places her at 11 St Andrews Terrace, a widow aged sixty-seven. Next door at no. 14 is Henry Kelland (the shop sign spells it Kalland), a sweep; he is giving notice of his intention of moving to 40 Wood Street where the 1894 directory lists him as a shopkeeper. He is still at 40 Wood Street in 1901 aged seventy-four living with Ann, his wife, aged sixty-four. No. 41a Wood Street is described as Kelland's Buildings which is occupied by a further eight people. The old thatched shops were demolished in the 1890s.

Opposite, bottom: Station Road, *c.* 1908. In the distance is the Ashton Temperance Hotel, one of five such businesses in the town at the time. The Royal Mail, built in 1861, is at the junction of Canal Road. The gabled building is H.E. Tucker's general stores, which was removed in the 1920s to create Priory Bridge Road. Carlton Terrace is left (see page 29) with the North End Stationery Depot on the corner of Belvedere Road.

Portman Street, c. 1906. John Brice, a British subject born in Germany, recorded this and many other side-street views between 1904 and 1910. Initially a newsagent in St James Street, Brice moved to 15a Station Road in about 1904 where his newsagent's shop shared the premises with Paul and Westlake, grocers. A better situation was soon found at 5 Whitehall Terrace, Station Road, where Brice remained in business until around 1916.

South Street, c. 1904. This view shows Highclere Terrace, eight residential properties opposite the Eagle Tavern Inn. In the distance beyond Highclere House is the chimney of the Somerset Manufacturing Co. Collar Works. In the 1970s this small industrial area also housed Frederick Theak and Co., tie works, and Stevens and Co., cardboard box manufacturers. The fine gas lamp in the foreground stands at the junction of Union Street, now Trinity Road. The former name denoted access to the old Union Workhouse, later called Trinity Hospital. A road sweeper is gradually working his way up South Street Hill.

Tauntfield Terrace, South Road, *c*. 1904. The terrace was built to accommodate the business entrepreneurs of the day. The large house in the foreground, Haldane, was home to piano and organ dealer Frederick W. Baker. He lived here with his wife and five children with mother's help and servant Lucy Crockford. Next door was Herbert Hawkes of Hawkes, ironmonger and agricultural dealer, in East Street. He had one child and one domestic servant. Further along was Henry Stevens, tailor, another Taunton employer.

Billetfield House, *c*. 1905. The building has a prominent tower which still exists; however, the arched entrance is no longer present. At this time Mansfield Road did not exist. Billet Street gave access down to East Street only. The property was for sale in 2007 for around £500,000 as Wessex Lodge, described as an imposing building of 4,030sq ft with car parking.

The Crescent, *c.* 1917. The foundation stone for the Crescent was laid in 1807 by William Kinglake. A Catholic chapel was built in 1822; this became the Masonic Hall. The Crescent Fields were a large amenity feature but County Hall was built here in 1935. The old police station at the southern edge was demolished in 1963 and further county offices were built in what remained of the field.

Vivary Park and surrounding area, *c.* 1930. In the early 1900s the bandstand was used by the military depot band and also that of the Great Western Railway. Taunton was the depot of the 13th Regimental District and headquarters of the Second Somerset Volunteer Battalion and West Somerset Imperial Yeomanry Cavalry. The great brick keep of Jellalabad Barracks, seen in the picture, was built in 1878.

Castle Green, *c.* 1950. The Castle Hotel, formerly two storeys high, now has three. The fourth was added in 1965 and the 100-year-old wisteria still thrives. This whole area originally served as a livestock market until 1929 (see page 55). In earlier times the area served as the outer castle ward and was surrounded by a moat and defences, including the raised area upon which stands the Municipal Buildings.

French Weir, *c.* 1904. The park was formed when the old canal was filled up with town refuse in the 1890s. The horse chestnuts were planted in 1898 and swings installed in 1903. A bathing station had been established on the river. Ladies were allowed on Mondays, Wednesdays and Fridays from 7 a.m. until 12 p.m., gentlemen at other times including Sunday from 6.00 a.m. to 8.30 a.m. Season tickets were sold for 5*s* first class, 3½*s* second class.

Above: Thomas Street, *c.* 1904. The street housed working class families and the 1901 Census gives an interesting insight into late Victorian social history. Nos 3 to 32 Thomas Street housed fifty-eight males and sixty-five females, an average of just over four people per household. Of the male workers nine worked for the GWR. Other professions included carpenter, postman, blacksmith and hairdresser. The youngest worker was a fourteen-year-old dressmaker's apprentice.

No. 2 Laburnum Street, *c.* 1907. Emily Jane Coleman (aged thirty-eight in 1901) stands with her son Stanley. The house was built in 1901 and bought by the tenants for £795 in 1947. Emily's daughter Ada is pictured on page 84.

Laburnum Street, *c.* 1903. The street was one of many being built around the town at this time. The working class at last had the opportunity to buy their own houses. A newly built house in the street could be obtained for £200, with a £50 deposit. The road has yet to be surfaced.

Stephen Street, *c.* 1903. The houses are almost identical in style and construction to those seen above. Over one hundred years later they have admirably stood the test of time. What could be said of today's estates? Apart from residential property Stephen Street was also home to Stevens and Co., box makers and printers' works.

Bridge Street, *c.* 1900. To the left are the premises of Henry J. Spiller. This building business was started in Taunton by Henry's father, John. Henry James Spiller was twice mayor of Taunton, a magistrate and market trustee. The company were responsible for building many of the town's more prominent buildings, including the reconstruction of St James's church tower from 1871 to 1873, Hatcher and Sons' new shop at 54 and 55 High Street (1894), Fox, Fowler and Co.'s bank and the St James Street Electricity Works. Mr R.G. Spiller succeeded to the business after moving to Chard in 1910. After his death in 1955 the family business passed to his son in law Mr Durie. Mr Durie's son and grandsons still run the firm.

Shops at Carlton Terrace, *c.* 1906. The terrace stands between Belvedere Road and Albemarle Road. Right to left, the first shop is J. Chilcott baker, at no. 1, lately removed from Albemarle Road. W. Morgan's antique furniture shop comes next then Cecil Dawkins' new music store at number three. Featured in *Taunton Revisited*, Mr Dawkins had worked for Collard and Collard in North Street and lived at Malvern Terrace.

North Town, *c.* 1844. This is a painting by Thomas Ellis Manning (1803–82). The artist was born in Exeter. It is difficult to say precisely where this is. The most likely location would be Bridge Street or Station Road. There is a gate in the road which is unusual. Apart from the pictures by Harry Frier, views of the town from this era are very rare.

2

Transport

Double-decker trams, photographed by W.H. Stone in 1903. The trams are standing on the passing loop between Albemarle Road and Belvedere Road. These cars were built on Brush A1 trucks. They seated twenty-two in the lower saloon and twenty-nine on the top deck. The entire fleet of six double-deckers was sold to Leamington and Warwick Tramways in 1905. They were replaced by six single-deck cars built by Brush and seating twenty-four. During this changeover period the system was closed for two months while the entire track was re-laid on granite setts.

Lyng Halt, *c.* 1962. Athelney junction is in the far distance. The little station opened in 1928 but remained a single-track as it was bypassed by a new track from Althelney to Cogload. The photograph has been taken from the road bridge.

Athelney station and signal-box, *c.* 1960. The station opened in 1853 and closed in 1964. From here a single line led back to Lyng Halt but the route to Taunton lay via Durston and Cogload junction. Onward from Athelney was Curry Rivel junction. Left led to Langport East and Castle Cary while Yeovil was reached via Langport West on the right. Previously subject to flooding the line between Athelney and Curry Rivel junction was raised when the track was doubled. The wooden station building is now at Stoke St Gregory playing fields.

Creech Halt, 1928. The smoke in the photograph is from the first train to use the station on 13 August 1928. The chimney belonged to the paper mills. Built at a cost of around £600, the station had a brick built waiting room and award winning platform gardens. The station closed in October 1964. The structure in the foreground is a wind operated pump designed to remove water from the track.

Thornfalcon station from the north, 1962. This was the first station on the Chard line beyond Creech Sidings. Originally named Thorne Falcon and with wooden platforms the station became Thornfalcon in 1902. The station opened in 1871 and at some point concrete platforms replaced the old wooden ones. The line was closed in 1962.

Engine no. 82044 at Taunton station with the 9.45 a.m. to Yeovil, 1967. The station opened in 1842 with the arrival of the engine *Castor* and a long train of carriages. The station has seen many changes over the years including the removal of its all-over roof in the 1930s. Two bridges cross Station Road. One carries the main line and platforms, the other the goods avoiding loop.

Bishops Lydeard station, looking towards Taunton, *c.* 1908. The station opened in 1862 and the Up platform on the left was added in 1906. Minehead was not reached until 1874. In 1882 500 men worked in gangs of seventy along the entire 22½ miles of track to convert it from broad to standard gauge, a project which took only two days. GWR assumed control in 1897 and the opening of Butlin's Holiday Camp in 1962 added to the summertime holiday passenger trade. Despite this British Rail considered the line to be uneconomical and closed it down in 1971. The line is now under the control of the private West Somerset Rail Company.

Hatch station, *c.* 1910. This is the Down view towards the signal-box and road bridge. This view differs from earlier photographs as the sleepers have been re-laid at shorter intervals. The line from Creech to Chard opened in 1866 and entered a 154yd tunnel on the Up side of the station. Final closure of the line came in 1964.

Milverton station, *c.* 1915. Work on the railway from Norton Fitzwarren to Wiveliscombe started shortly after the Devon and Somerset Railway Act of 1864. Excavations commenced at Ford Bridge in October 1865. The first train carrying directors and shareholders ran through Milverton on 21 February 1871. The boys from the local school were let out to see it. The official opening of the line to Wiveliscombe took place on 8 June 1871 and was marked by a general holiday. In late July 1871 regular cheap excursions to Weston-super-Mare were on offer. The line from Norton to Milverton was doubled in 1937 mostly as a result of Ilfracombe excursion traffic. Like many branch lines the system closed in the mid-1960s.

Wiveliscombe station, *c.* 1905. The Devon and Somerset Railway Act was passed in 1864. The section from Norton Fitzwarren to Wiveliscombe opened on 8 June 1871. In the next two years the section from Wiveliscombe to Barnstaple was completed, later giving connections to Lynton, Ilfracombe and Torrington. An extension south to Exeter completed the circle. The standard gauge conversion took place in 1881 and the line was absorbed by the GWR in 1901. The system closed in 1966 and the station is now used as industrial buildings. The very last train to run through the station was a 'last train excursion' from Barnstaple Junction to Taunton and back, organised by Barnstaple Round Table to run on 1 October 1966.

Opposite, top: Durston station, *c.* 1962. The station opened in 1853 on the main line from Taunton to Bridgwater. At Durston Junction a single track led to Lyng and Athelney. The main line crossed the River Parrett at Somerset Bridge, an area often subject to flooding. The station closed in October 1964.

Opposite, bottom: Norton Fitzwarren station, *c.* 1960. Originally a two-track station with single Up and Down platforms, it opened in 1873. When the line was quadrupled, this layout was replaced by two island platforms and the timber buildings shown in the photograph. At the station close to the Railway Hotel a single track led to the Minehead Branch, now preserved as the West Somerset Railway. The station closed in 1961.

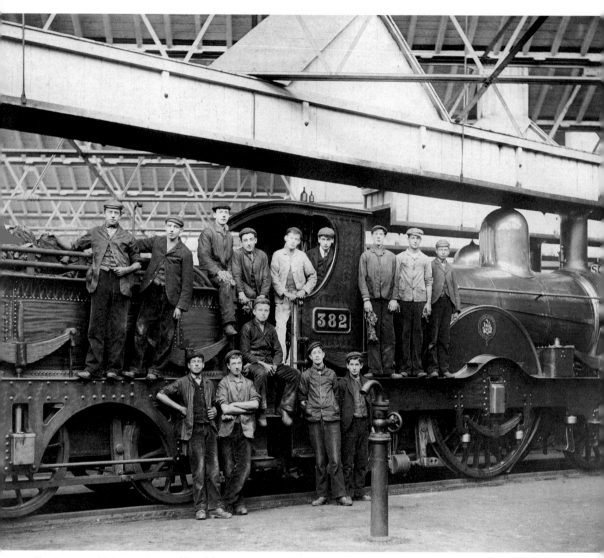

Engine no. 382, *c.* 1898. This GWR locomotive was photographed inside the newly constructed engine shed. The locomotive is a 'Sir Daniel' Class 2–2–2 built at Swindon in 1866. She was re-boilered in 1890 and finally withdrawn from service in March 1903. The young men, some with cleaning rags, appear to be apprentices or cleaners.

Opposite, top: Leyland Lion bus, *c.* 1930. The registration of the vehicle dates to 1927–8. In February 1929 the GWR and National Omnibus Company jointly formed the Western National Omnibus Company and the new company commenced business in May. The Leyland Lion was one of the best-known buses of the day. Often the chassis would long outlast the bodywork and numerous adaptations of the former buses took place. The 1930 LT2 version had a 29hp petrol engine, four-speed crash gearbox, semi-floating rear axle and vacuum brakes.

Opposite, bottom: Double-decker bus, *c.* 1965. The massive wall topped by the engine shed was built in 1895. This was constructed of Devonian limestone from Westleigh Quarry. During the 1940s an engine is said to have run through the wall of the shed to overhang Station Road. This bridge in the picture carries the main line through Taunton station.

Lorry crash, 1979. This photograph gave rise to the classic newspaper caption 'Driver has close shave'. B&S driver Ernie Roberts lost control of his vehicle in Finsbury Park where it jack-knifed into a barber's shop and ended up looking like it was coming out. Ernie was unhurt but his load of fertiliser caused a jam in busy Seven Sisters Road for most of the day. B&S Express Freight was founded by Brian Bunney and his partner in 1970. *(Brian Bunney)*

National bus in Corporation Street, *c.* 1923. This is an early model as it still retains solid tyres. Dennis, one of the main bus manufacturers, introduced pneumatic tyres on single-deckers in 1925. Originally the private motor bus 'Lady Betty' ran from Corporation Street from 1914 to 1920. She was operated by Mr Ireland, a well-known local carrier.

Charabanc, *c.* 1914. This appears to be a works photograph as the vehicle is still unregistered. It was constructed for Mr B.E. Dening, proprietor of the Taunton Motor Company. Taunton had to do without its charabancs during the First World War as most were converted to trucks and used for the war effort. In happier times hundreds of people were conveyed to the seaside, Gough's Caves, Wincanton races and local beauty spots.

Hatcher's delivery van, *c.* 1932. This Leyland was first registered to Hatcher's in April 1931. The company remains one of the town's longest-running businesses; it originated in 1788 as a linen drapery started by Matthew Colman.

Single-decker tram, *c.* 1906. These two photographs illustrate trams near the terminus at either end of the system. Here the tram sits on the track just before the acute curve into the depot at the end of East Reach. These single-deckers replaced the original double-deck cars in 1905. Judging by the new condition of the car and the interest shown this is likely to be the tram's first run after temporary closure of the system in 1905.

Single-decker tram, *c.* 1909. Originally the system which opened in 1901 ended at Taunton station. In August 1909 a further extension was added which carried the tramway along Kingston Road to its junction with Salisbury Street. To the left is the junction with Greenway Road. Taunton Fire Brigade has installed a ladder by the lamp post for emergency rescue purposes. Compared with the view above, the car has acquired a few advertising boards in the intervening few years.

Bridgwater and Taunton Canal, *c.* 1905. This view of work being done was taken at Creech St Michael. Essentially the canal was a branch of the Grand Western Canal which it joined just north of the towpath bridge at Firepool Lock. By 1838 it was possible for tug boats to make the journey by canal from Tiverton to Huntworth. Three years later the canal was connected to the new floating harbour at Bridgwater and in 1842 the Chard Canal opened, although this was never a commercial success.

The canal and road bridge, Creech, *c.* 1910. This postcard was issued by William T. Brass, baker and confectioner at Creech. Through the bridge arch can be seen the doorway in the photograph above. After the closure of the Somerset section of the Grand Western Canal the Bridgwater and Taunton branch gradually declined in use until the final commercial barge ran in 1907. Today it is a valuable resource for flood control, walkers and anglers.

Motor car in Fore Street, 1903. The vehicle was unregistered as registration only became compulsory the following year. A view of things to come occurred in 1897 when Taunton saw its first motor car. This was the 4hp Autocar that was driven the length of the country by journalist Henry Sturmey. The car was primarily developed in France, Germany and America, Victorian Britain having a strange aversion to its presence. This was typified by the Red Flag Act which required that a man walked in front of the vehicle waving a red flag. This was repealed in 1896 and the speed limit increased to a dizzy 12mph. In 1900 the Automobile Club of Great Britain and Ireland held its famous 1,000-mile trial which took in most of the cities of England and Scotland.

In Taunton, motor engineers like James Beach and Charles Allen, helped establish a fledging motor industry in the town. Several local businessmen, for example the photographer Henry Montague Cooper, were early car owners. He had a De-Dion two-seater in 1903.

Chapman's delivery carriage, 1900. This is a works photograph from the Railway Carriage and Wagon Company Ltd. Originally these carriages were drawn by horses but later traction engines were employed. Chapman's also used steam lorries and acquired a fleet of Leyland motor vehicles in the early 1920s.

Peveril of the Peak, 1908. Early views of locomotives at Taunton are relatively rare. Some were issued as postcards by the London bookseller E. Pouteau in about 1905 but this photograph and *Lightning* on page 46 were from a private album. Larger locomotives were being employed by the GWR and alterations to accommodate them were made to the platforms and line in 1907.

Lightning at Taunton station, 1908. This 3001 Class engine no. 3016 was built as a 2–2–2 locomotive at Swindon in 1892. She was a standard gauge engine, double-framed with 7ft 8½in driving wheels. The class proved unsteady at high speed owing to the combination of a heavy front end and a long rigid wheelbase. Following a derailment of no. 3021 in Box Tunnel in 1893, alterations were made in 1894 to include a reconstruction to 4–2–2 by adding leading bogies. *Lightning*, the third engine of that name for GWR, was withdrawn in 1911.

Taunton shed, April 1934. No. 4926 has been stripped for repainting. The engine shed opened in 1896 and was 180sq ft in area. The shed contained twenty-eight engine pits and a central turntable which could be operated by two men.

3

Shopping & Working

Parade Market, *c.* 1900. The market took place on Wednesdays and Saturdays.
Its affairs were overseen by sixty Market Trustees, including many of the important
businessmen in the town. Two fairs were also held, the Town Fair in June and North
Town Fair in July. In this view can be seen a large assortment of local pottery wares.
Meat and vegetables were sold in the Victorian Rooms, left, which housed a British
Restaurant during the war and was demolished in 1963. The Corn Exchange, centre,
opened as a fish market in 1854 and was demolished in 1937 after housing
Taunton's first cinema, the Exchange, which locals referred to unkindly as
'The Bughouse'.

Adams' cake factory, Railway Street, *c.* 1900. Older Tauntonians still refer to the steep part of the street as 'Cake Hill'. Herbert Adams, who owned the factory, was born in North Newton in about 1860. In 1901 he was living at 1 Ash Villa at Rowbarton with his wife Eliza. They had seven children and employed two servants. The eldest son, also Herbert, worked in the cake factory.

Opposite, top: Taunton telephone exchange, *c.* 1920. A proposal to establish a telephone exchange in Taunton in 1889 failed as the twenty necessary subscribers could not be found. By 1902 the National Telephone Co. Ltd were operating an exchange with fifty-four subscribers, nearly all commercial. There were two public call offices, one in Hammet Street, the company's own offices, and another at the Royal Mail Inn in Station Road.

Opposite, bottom: Taunton telephone exchange, *c.* 1925. Note the numbers posted up for the police, fire and ambulance. Early telephones were a cumbersome affair containing batteries and a crank-handled magneto. All calls went via the operator in the exchange.

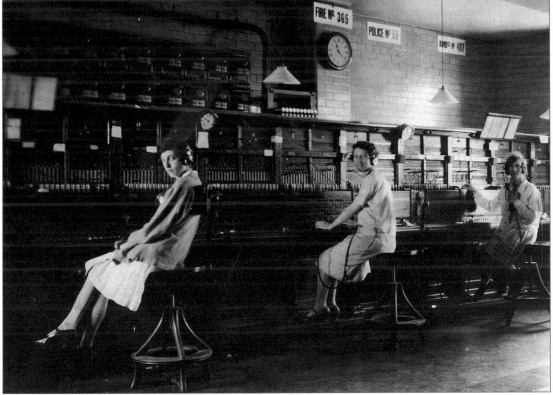

Filling barrels inside the Taunton Cider works at Norton Fitzwarren, *c.* 1930. In the early nineteenth century the Revd Thomas Cornish started selling the cider he made at Heathfield Rectory. Nearly a century later Arthur Moore and George Pallet formed a cider-making business at Norton.

Filled barrels in the factory yard, Taunton Cider, *c.* 1930. The company was formed in 1921, initially employing just six workers who produced some 10,000 gallons of cider a year.

A view of the Taunton Cider factory from the main road, *c.* 1930. The 1950s and '60s saw expansion and technological advances. Quantock Vale and Ashford Vale as well as Bruttons and Horrells were acquired. Pasteurising technologies were introduced and this enabled the product to travel and to keep for longer. Kegs were introduced and handling procedures improved with the introduction of fork-lift trucks.

Another view of the yard and one of the delivery lorries at Taunton Cider, *c.* 1930. Around this time larger presses were introduced together with increased vattage, cellarage and bottling stores covering nearly 4 acres. At its height in the early 1990s the company employed over 500 people. In 1995 Matthew Clark took over Taunton Cider but withdrew from Norton Fitzwarren in 1998. The company has now re-branded as part of the multinational Constellation Brands Group. Gaymer Cider Company of Shepton Mallet still produces some of the old Taunton Cider beverages.

Kingston Road Cycle Depot, *c.* 1910. The man in the photograph is John Godwin who also owned the music shop in the foreground. J. Godwin is listed in directories at Havelock Cottage, Kingston Road, in 1906 and the Cycle Depot appears from 1910 to 1919. No trace of the music shop was found so it was probably a very short-lived business.

Opposite: Goodhind and Co., 40 East Street, *c.* 1953. John Goodhind started the business in the 1870s. The previous owner was Robert Green and John Goodhind was employed as the manager. The company continued to trade under the Goodhind name although the owner in the 1950s was Sidney Smith. They traded as wine and spirit merchants, shippers and bonders. The company's stone spirit jars in the 1890s featured as a trademark a man's head on a hind's body. By the early 1960s the business had become known as Tyler and Co. Ltd.

Mr A.E. de Breffe's antique shop, *c.* 1915. Mr de Breffe learnt the furniture trade with Taunton furnishers Lawrence and Thompson. He set up his own antique shop in 1912 but moved to these premises in Fore Street two years later. The building now houses the Portman Building Society (see also page 60).

Below: J. Manning and Son, *c.* 1910. Mr Manning opened his monumental works in Station Road in about 1875. The company produced chimney pieces, monuments, headstones, marble washstand tops, counter tops, fenders and baths. All sorts of monumental engraving was also undertaken.

Taunton livestock market, *c.* 1905. This view shows the cattle pens which stood inside a wall on what is now the car park behind the Municipal Buildings. The market was held on Saturdays and moved in 1929 to its current site at Priory Bridge Road. As 2007 dawned it was announced that the market would move to Bridgwater, ending Taunton's centuries-long status as a market town.

Taunton livestock market, *c.* 1905. The sheep pens were next to the Castle Museum. W.R.J. Greenslade was a Market Trustee in the 1920s. His auctioneering business dated back to the 1850s when it traded as Greenslade and Son. Originally the firm also involved itself with wholesale and imported wines and spirits. Stoneware jars exist marked 'Greenslade and Son Trull and Taunton'. The company became R.N. Greenslade in about 1870 then Greenslade and Kidner before becoming W.R.J. Greenslade and Co. Now trading as Greenslade, Taylor, Hunt, the company is still heavily involved in Taunton market activities.

The Country Mails, *c.* 1904. This view is of the main Taunton post office in Church Square. This was open from 7 a.m. until 10 p.m. weekdays, also on Sundays for two hours for telegraph business. A new post office was built by Pollard and Son of Bridgwater in North Street; it opened in 1911.

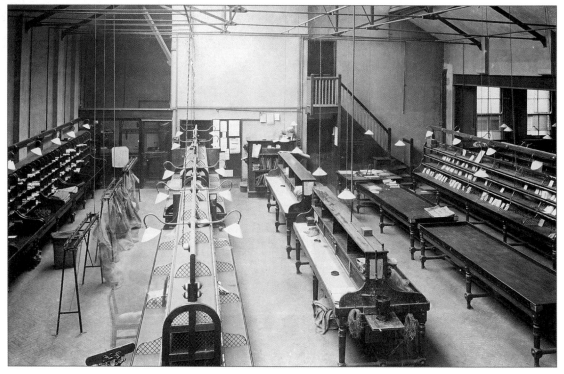

The sorting office, *c.* 1915. In 1903 Taunton had a very efficient letter collection and delivery service. There were nineteen wall letter-boxes which were cleared seven times daily. Deliveries from various parts occurred at 7 a.m., 9 a.m., 11 a.m., 2.15 p.m. and lastly at 7.30 p.m. There was a 7 a.m. Sunday delivery with letters from all parts of the country.

E. Kerslake, baker, *c.* 1902. Mr Kerslake is shown with his delivery cart which appears to have been pushed by hand. His bakery was at 143 East Reach on the junction with South Street. The town had twenty-eight bakers at this time, and most of the local villages also had a resident baker. Emmanuel Kerslake was born in Halberton, Devon, in about 1870. His wife Sabina was born in Canada. The boy is probably Walter White, baker's assistant, who lived with Mr Kerslake as a lodger.

C. Allen and Son, *c*. 1904. This view shows the junction of Wood Street with Bridge Street and the Tone Bridge Foundry and Engineering Works, originally acquired by Allen's in the 1870s. Within the next few years Charles Allen developed the business into a motor repair works and by the 1920s was importing Chevrolets from America. The mock Tudor showrooms were built in 1928. During the 1960s the company distributed Jaguar, Daimler, Rover and Vauxhall cars together with Land Rover, Bedford and Scammell commercials.

Arthur Martin's Autorama, *c*. 1970. Few could miss this high-profile business at 78–88 East Reach, which was part of Southville Motors Ltd. A day and night A38 service was offered. This included petrol, oil, tyres, batteries and accessories together with a coffee cabin, wash and brush-up rooms, toilet and rest area.

Madame Jaques, 7 Albemarle Terrace, *c.* 1906. Mrs Jaques was a dressmaker by trade and she opened this shop in about 1904. The shop was situated on the corner of Albemarle Road and Station Road and offered high-class ladies and children's dressmaking, as well as 'own materials made up, fit and style guaranteed'.

The Electricity Showrooms, 1917. These were situated at 1 St James Street. New showrooms opened on the site of the old Corn Exchange in 1937. On the table is the first Tricity cooking set.

A.F. Loxston, hairdressers, *c.* 1910. This shop was at 5 Kingston Road. The fine window display advertises Carbolic Tooth Powder, Capstan Cigarettes and tobacco and a product called Kolene. Arthur Frank Loxston started work aged fourteen as an office boy when living at 28 Thomas Street. His father Isaac worked on the GWR.

Fore Street, *c.* 1955. The building in the centre is the Tudor Restaurant said to be the oldest domestic building in Taunton. The building for many years housed Halliday's Antique shop which F.G. Halliday acquired in 1909 when the West Somerset Stores closed. Blake's Medical Stores was previously A.E. de Breffe's antique shop (shown on page 54).

J. White, corn and seed merchant, *c.* 1910.
The shop was at 6 Shuttern. The building is still
much the same but all the chimney pots are gone.
John White was born at Halberton in 1851.
He owned mills at Staplegrove where he was
assisted by his son Frederick.

Below: The entrance to Bathpool Mills, *c.* 1925.
It is likely that a mill has existed on this part of
the River Tone for many centuries. The mill
buildings were badly damaged by fire in 1812 and
in 1891. They were rebuilt but fire struck again in
1915. The mill was only partially rebuilt this time
and the damaged areas were demolished in the
1920s. An undamaged part remained and this is
still used by small businesses. The once-elegant
mill house is now used by Westwood Fencing as a
fence panel factory. All the interior walls have
been demolished and a flat roof has been added.

Franklin and Hare Ltd, *c.* 1925. This company was one of Taunton's oldest jewellers. The business was founded by a Mr Lendon before 1800. Mr Lendon's two sons and daughter ran the business until it was bought by Mr C. Haddon who introduced quality watchmaking. This section of the shop at 28 Fore Street was added to the original no. 29 after 1900.

Franklin and Hare Ltd, *c.* 1925. This smaller section of the store next to the Corn Exchange was the original shop. In the 1880s the company was known as Haddon and Franklin but became Franklin and Hare in about 1897. The business expanded in the 1890s to include the production of spectacles for the hospital and local oculists. Eventually the shop had twelve separate showrooms.

Interior of the main part of Franklin and Hare's shop, *c.* 1925. This was lit by electricity in the 1890s. At the 1901 Census one of the partners, Herbert Hare, lived on the shop premises, while the other, Thomas Franklin, had a house at 16 Mount Street. This he shared with his wife Louisa, daughter Grace, a cook and a housemaid.

The sports and trophy section, Franklin and Hare, *c.* 1925. Note the various wicker picnic hampers on the floor. The company ceased trading in the mid-1960s after 160 years in business.

Taunton Cooperative's original store, 1889.
The society was registered in March 1889 and the
shop opened at 1 Magdalene Street on 16 May.
At the first meeting in November 1889 at Paul
Street Coffee Tavern the first balance sheet
showed sales of £984 with a £69 surplus. The
membership amounted to 200. In 1891 a bakery
was added and by 1892 membership had
increased to 425.

Below: Taunton Cooperative's new store, 1894.
This new store replaced the original store in
March 1894. Also in Magdalene Street, it offered
a greater range of products including boots and
shoes, ironmongery and tin ware. By June 1895
clothing, hats and drapery were added and
membership stood at 1,150. A branch store
opened at Rowbarton in 1901 and Wiveliscombe
in 1922.

Cooperative Society, East Street frontage, *c.* 1928. The premises on the right were previously the studio of photographer Henry Montague Cooper. In 1929 the company's sales amounted to £151,500 and membership stood at 5,340.

Cooperative Society, East Street, 1937. Growth for the company continued rapidly and membership stood at 7,250 in 1936. The new emporium was officially opened by the president Mr W.J. Hodges on 24 April 1937. The new building covered an area of 11,500sq ft with a frontage to East Street of 67ft.

Cooperative Society drapery department, 1937. A tobacco kiosk was situated on the left-hand side of the arcade at the entrance to the store. Once inside the emporium there was immediate access to the drapery, gents' outfitting and tailoring and gents' footware.

Cooperative Society food hall entrance, 1937. The food hall stood at the rear of the main emporium on the ground floor. Both could also be accessed at the rear of the premises from Magdalene Street.

Cooperative Society food hall interior, 1937. This area contained fruit stalls and a modern display unit in the centre. The old grocery shop in Magdalene Street was converted into a warehouse and dispatch section with a spacious loading and receiving dock.

Cooperative Society ladies' hats department, 1937. This was on the upper floor with a view over East Street.

Cooperative Society furnishing department, 1937. The department was extensive and well lit. All the lighting in the store was installed by Henry West and Son, 31 High Street, Taunton. The very angular, chunky style of the furniture is typical of the 1930s.

Cooperative Society garage, 1937. This was situated in Magdalene Street. The company also operated its own fleet of delivery vans. My father was a driver for the Co-op in the 1950s and 1960s and as a small child I used to accompany him on his midweek run to Watchet. During the 1960s the store increased its frontage, taking in an umbrella shop, confectioner and Hodges the newsagent. In 1999 the premises were closed and converted to a new store for Primark, which opened in April 2000.

4

People & Events

An aerial view of the Tone Bridge and Bridge Street during the 1960 floods. In
October 1960 the Tone Valley, including Taunton, suffered a severe flood. The villages
of Bathpool, Ruishton and Creech St Michael were badly affected together with the
Somerset Levels and Moors. In Taunton 360 houses, shops and business premises
were flooded; damage amounted to £114,000.

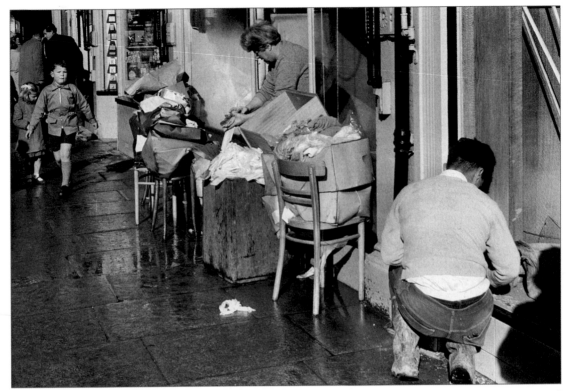

Clearing up in Bridge Street after the 1960 floods. One of the shops to suffer most was Messrs Paul and Hooper's North Town Stores. The stores lost about £20,000 worth of stock and suffered the heaviest damage. Most of this occurred in the large wholesale department at the rear. Many tons of goods, including a large amount of Christmas stock, had to be written off and dumped. Clearing up went on all weekend with some ninety people working on it, many during the night. During all this time the firm's travellers still maintained normal deliveries to customers.

Of course none of us youngsters went to school on this day during the flood. I remember walking down Bridge Street and we all held hands to cross the road opposite the cinema. The bigger vehicles created a bow wave which smashed shop windows, but there was little sign of looting.

The tractor is a David Brown owned by Henson and Sons of Trull. The Labour Exchange at 13 Bridge Street was demolished in later years to widen access into Wood Street. Next door are the offices of the *Somerset County Herald*.

The junction of Wood Street and Bridge Street during the flood. At one point the bridge beyond was considered at risk because timber from the adjacent yard dammed up behind the bridge supports. In the late 1960s work began on the Tone Valley Scheme which modified the channel of the river. The original flood walls and embankments of the Tone through Taunton were further updated in the 1980s.

Above: This is the Odeon cinema, which was built as the Lyceum in 1913 on the site of the George Inn. The building became the Classic cinema and was demolished in 1998 to make way for Laverock Court. Les Laverock was the former cinema manager. The Esso garage has now been developed into small shops and the residential Belvedere Gardens.

Athelney floods, *c.* 1960. In the centre is Athelney crossing; the small station building can also be seen. Just beyond the railway line is the old Athelney engine house. The course of the river here is artificial with high embankments to control flooding. A breach in the embankment (shown on page 73) occurred just out of view at the bottom of the picture in 1929. This led to serious flooding in the area. The island in the distance is Athelney Hill, which has a memorial to King Alfred.

Curload floods, 1929. Immediately on the left is the breach in the embankment responsible for the flooding. Local people, including the Uphams, repaired the damage with sandbags. An unknown photographer travelled the area by boat and issued a series of at least fifteen postcards showing the extent of the floods and damage inflicted.

Curload floods, 1929. W.J. Upham inspects the damage done to his withy business. W.J. Upham senior was described as a wicker chair maker in the 1901 Census. Other occupations at Curload connected with the withy business in 1901 were withy stripper, withy grower and withy whitener. Withy products are still made in the area. Products supplied in 1914 included white, brown and buff withies together with green plait.

Fire and flood at Pollards timber yard, 1889. Both of the illustrations on this page come from the *Illustrated London News* of 16 March 1889. The newspaper sent an artist to Taunton to record the scenes.

Floods in Bridge Street, 1889. The Telegraph Inn is on the right and the George Inn in the centre. Heavy rain over two days resulted in serious flooding from Bristol to Exeter. Further north, the Forest of Dean was also affected. A train was stranded between Durston and Creech when its boiler fire was extinguished. A fire engine had to pump flood water away to release it.

Wind damage at Galmington, 1990. Several of the flats off College Way, Galmington, were damaged by high winds. The upper balconies caught the strong gusts of wind and the flat roofs were completely lifted off. When the roofs were replaced they had strengthening purlins.

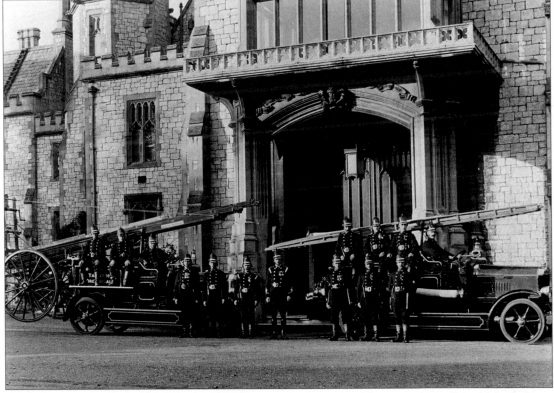

Taunton Fire Brigade at Shire Hall, c. 1925. One senses that the appliances seen in this photograph are quite new. The Taunton Fire Brigade was quite late in changing from horse-drawn to motor appliances. In 1902 the station was in Magdalene Street, where it remained until a new station opened at Lisieux Way. The 1902 brigade consisted of two officers, a foreman, turncock and ten fireman. In about 1900 the Lieutenant, Mr A.G. Palmer, was connected to the National Telephone Exchange. Before this the brigade was summoned by a messenger. Rural callers had to rely on a telegram. Seven fire appliance boxes were stationed around the town with names of key holders living nearby listed on them. Somerset County Fire Brigade was formed in 1948.

Radiac Factory at Pool Wall, *c.* 1950. This entrance was off the High Street. It seems likely that the ladies are assembled for a coach trip which the company ran occasionally. Bournemouth was the destination in July 1954. For young girls wages at the factory were better than those in a shop – less than £2 a week at this time.

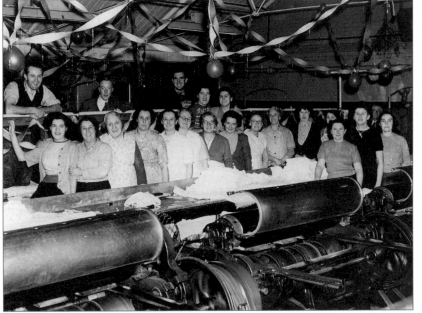

Radiac Factory, *c.* 1953. In the picture are Eddie Coleman, Maud Coleman, Phyllis Smale, Florence Council, Mrs Coles and Lily Hearn. The decorations are possibly for the coronation. Before the 1860s there was a silk factory on the site after which linen collars were produced by Young and Co. This became Taunton Manufacturing Co. in 1892 and finally Radiac. The factory closed in 1958 and the area was redeveloped.

Obridge rail crash, 1907. These two photographs illustrate the importance of postcards as conveyors of news. The photograph below was actually posted on the day of the accident, 30 April, while this one was posted the day after. It was possible for a local photographer to take, print and sell postcards within the space of a few hours. It would also be possible for the card to be delivered the same day if it was posted early enough.

Obridge rail crash, 1907. GWR engine no. 537 was hauling a Chard passenger train of four carriages when it was struck a glancing blow by an Exeter goods locomotive shunting at Obridge. Three of the passenger carriages were wrecked and seven passengers injured. The goods locomotive was derailed and badly damaged. It is believed that the gentleman with the beard is the driver of no. 537, Mr F. Oram of Chard. His tank engine, an 0–4–2 built in 1868, was removed to Taunton shed for repairs and continued in service until 1932.

The Yarde family at Staplehay, *c.* 1918. Rose Cottage on the right can also be seen in the distance on page 97. The man in the doorway is my grandfather Albert Henry Yarde, born in Buckland St Mary in 1887, and lately returned from the First World War. Next to him is his wife Mabel (née Mutter) whom he married at Trull in 1910. The two ladies by the wall are Jane Parsons (right), Albert Henry's aunt, and his mother-in-law Sara Mutter. The child on the wall is Charles Yarde, Albert's oldest son, born in 1912. The cottage was owned by William Mutter, Albert's father-in-law. Eight people were living in the cottage by 1920. Similar overcrowding led Albert Henry, one of eleven children, to be 'adopted' by his Aunt Jane who looked after him and his sister Mabel. It was not unusual in country areas for maiden aunts to take children from large families and bring them up as their own.

Foxhole Creech, *c.* 1918. On the left is Frank Rossiter with his mother Elizabeth in the background. The boy is Clifford Rossiter, born in 1910, and his sister Olive is seated on the horse.

Creech paper mill tug-of-war team, *c.* 1910. This event is taking place at the annual Creech St Michael Bazaar. There are swing boats in the distance. The paper mill opened in 1876 and was originally owned by R. Sommerville. It was taken over by Purnells in 1946 and the British Printing Corporation bought it in 1965. Eventually the business closed and its prominent chimney was demolished in the 1990s.

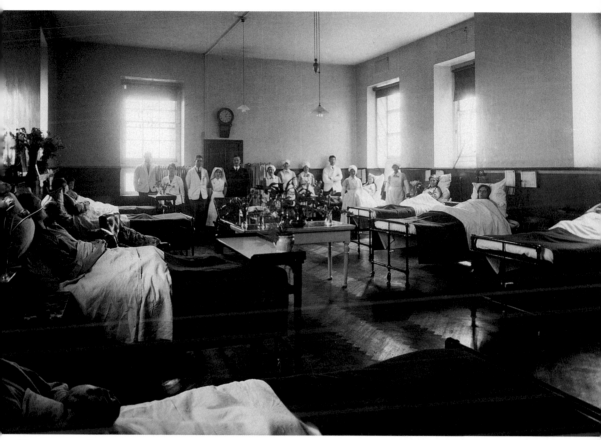

Taunton and Somerset Hospital, c. 1920. The writer of this uncaptioned card states that this is a photograph of Taunton Hospital 'taken some time ago'. The date of 1920 is a guess on my part. An early attempt to build a hospital in Taunton resulted in failure. The building was eventually sold as a private house and then in 1808 was converted to a convent (see page 117). In 1812 the centre block of a new hospital in East Reach opened. East and West wings were added in 1841/2, built with money given by the Tone Conservators. Further extensions were made in 1871/2 which increased the number of beds to 100. To commemorate Queen Victoria's Golden Jubilee in 1887 a Nursing Institute was built adjacent to the hospital's west wing. The institute had its own endowment so that it would be independent of the hospital. Over the doorway are the initials 'J.B.' They are those of the donor of £5,000 who wished to remain anonymous. The hospital site now contains offices and business premises as all medical facilities were transferred to Musgrove Hospital in 1987.

Opposite, top: Road mending, c. 1928. This shows work being done on the approach to the bridge at Bathpool. The ramps to the bridge were excavated from pits on either side of the bridge. During the early 1890s town refuse was used to refill the pits and this led to numerous complaints about the unsanitary conditions. Both pits were excavated by the author and his friends and a catalogue of the many bottles and pots found was assembled.

Opposite, bottom: By the canal at Bathpool, c. 1935. In the background is the corrugated-iron Iron Room. Haymaking on the bank are, left to right, Mr Dyer, Ada Dyer, Elizabeth Rossiter and Clifford Rossiter. The Iron Room served as a small church room immediately behind All Saints' Church. It was generally used as a community centre for the village until the Victory Village Hall opened at Monkton Heathfield after the Second World War.

West Monkton School Pageant, *c.* 1920. The school was built in 1845 and was designed to accommodate 163 children. After the First World War the government presented the parish with a large German field gun which was installed on a plinth in the school playground. The school moved to new premises in 1984 and the old buildings were demolished.

Harry Pring working on Tanpitts Farm, 1922. The binding machine is being drawn by Blossom, Prince and Smart. The machine could cut the standing corn and also tie it into sheaves.

Dedication of St Mary's memorial cross, *c.* 1920. In March 1919 the Revd Preb. Corfield of St Mary's presided over a meeting regarding the proposed memorial to men of the congregation who had fallen in the war. A design and location for the memorial were accepted at the meeting and it was agreed that the estimated cost of £500 would be raised by the parishioners. The cross was built of Doulting stone and inscribed to all men who lost their lives in the First World War.

Hestercombe, *c.* 1915. Second from the left is the Hon. Mrs Constance Portman, widow of E.W.B. Portman (1856–1911) of Hestercombe House. After her husband's death Mrs Portman stayed at Hestercombe until she died in 1951. It was said by the locals that it needed thirty people to keep a lady living in comfort. This included seven gardeners, a blacksmith, two laundry maids and the lodge keepers, who would be notified when the Hon Mrs Portman's car was due so that they could open the gates. E.W.B. Portman employed Edwin Lutyens to design formal gardens at the house between 1904 and 1906 with planting schemes by Gertrude Jekyll.

Fourth-prize carnival entry, *c.* 1911. The young lady is Ada Coleman who was brought up at 2 Laburnum Street. Her father was local hairdresser James Coleman whose shop was in Tancred Street. Ada's two elder brothers worked at the collar factory. The dress bears a photograph of King George V suggesting it was taken in the coronation year when Ada was nineteen years old. Camp Coffee was very popular with the working class. The formerly deferential servant featured on the label has gradually risen in status in these more enlightened years. Ada Coleman later married and became Ada Sellick; she is also featured on page 92 (the girl without flowers by the pillar).

First young women's Bible class 1896–1905. These serious young ladies attended class at the North Street Congregational Church. The chapel and part of the school premises were erected in 1842/3. Subsequent improvements took place and a house blocking the church from North Street was removed in 1884. Other activities included Sunday School, Band of Hope, Christian Endeavour and Penny Bank.

Peace celebrations conducted by Taunton Town Charity, 24 August 1945. This was one of a great many similar events that occurred shortly after VJ Day. The charity was an amalgamation of several local charities made by order of the Charity Commission in 1872. Initially its objects were to maintain endowed almshouses and pensions, subscribe to the hospital in respect of the sick poor and assist in the provision of recreation grounds and a public library.

Albemarle Baptist Chapel, *c.* 1906. It seems likely that the children of the chapel took part in the carnival procession on a regular basis as several different postcards exist. The chapel was built in 1875 by a group of members from the congregation at Silver Street. There were school premises behind the chapel and activities included a separate men and women's Bible class and a Sunday school.

Carnival group at Cotford Asylum, *c.* 1910. One assumes this to be the staff rather than the patients. The hospital was founded in 1897 and was better known in later years as Tone Vale Hospital. Since closure, the extensive grounds and buildings have been redeveloped into the village of Cotford St Luke, a process which is still ongoing. This postcard is by E.E. Cox, a professional photographer at 4 Albemarle Terrace from about 1905 until the mid-1920s when his address changed to 65 Station Road. Postcards were produced by Mr Cox throughout this time.

Lady cyclists in Vivary Park, *c.* 1905. Cycling became very popular in the 1880s and '90s, although the first lady cyclist was not seen in Taunton until 1888. Tricycles on which the elegant lady stood were popularised by such magazines as *The Lady's World* in the late 1880s. Later, a cycling costume of Dr Jaeger's hygienic woollen underwear, a divided petticoat or skirt, or knickerbockers under a skirt, were recommended, so that a respectable female cyclist remained womanly at all times.

Taunton County Cricket Ground, 1902. Somerset County Cricket Club first formed in 1875. Initially the club used Fulland's School as the Taunton venue, the idea being to travel around Somerset for fixtures. In 1881 Taunton Athletic Club opened a sports centre on Priory Fields adjacent to the River Tone. This soon became home to the county club. First class status was awarded in 1891 and in the late 1970s and early '80s the club enjoyed a golden era, winning five competitions. Currently plans are in hand for major improvements at the ground.

Feeding the pigeons at Vivary Park, *c.* 1907. The park gets its name from the Bishop of Winchester's vivarium. Two large ponds were established here by 1226 to store the Bishop's fish. In 1893 the borough bought the land from Dr Kinglake of Wilton House. The ornamental gates and bandstand were erected two years later and the fountain added in 1907.

Rowbarton Recreation Ground, *c.* 1910. The recreation ground was a gift of Thomas Penny who had developed the Greenway estate. It was opened by Mayoress Mrs Goodland on 8 June 1899. During the First World War the photographer Henry Montague Cooper took photographs of heavy guns and artillery in the park. Possibly it was used as a staging post before the guns were moved to the railway station.

John Hope Simpson's election as Member of Parliament for Taunton, 1922. These celebration scenes took place at the Municipal Buildings. Sir John Hope Simpson was born in 1868 and died in 1961, having served as Liberal MP for Taunton from 1922 to 1924. He is known for his work on the question of refugees. Port Hope Simpson, Newfoundland and Labrador, was named after him in response to the backing he had given to John Osborn Williams and the Labrador Development Company. The company exported pitprops to Cardiff for the collieries of South Wales.

Creech St Michael Drum and Fife Band, 1911. The photograph was taken by J.G. Mitchell in Creech churchyard during the coronation celebrations of King George V. John Mitchell was an amateur postcard publisher of some merit. He produced cards of the local villages from around 1907 to the 1920s. Like W.T. Brass he was a baker and was born at Creech in about 1878.

A lovely scene of two lady farm workers at Heathfield Farm, Creech St Michael, *c.* 1906. The Census and Trade Directory can give us a clue who they are. At the time the farm was owned by Walter John Heal. In 1901 he is listed by the census as living at Middlezoy with his wife, three young children and two sisters-in-law. The ladies are probably Walter's wife Annie (aged thirty-two) and one of her sisters, Carrie or Emily Thatcher, who were both in their early twenties. There are no clues to the name of the dog.

Taunton Carnival first prize, *c.* 1910. The hat alone must warrant a first prize for this French model. Another postcard shows the same girl as a dairy maid, although that entry only came second. Both cards were published by S.L. Owen who appears to be one of the many local amateurs producing postcards at the time. The 1901 Census lists Spencer Lewis Owen aged twenty-one, a grocer's assistant. He started producing postcards in about 1910.

Taunton Carnival entry, 1922. This fine submarine was built by the Royal Navy Pensioners' Society. The postcard was published by Spencer Lewis Owen who had a shop at 94 East Reach from 1914 to the 1920s.

Taunton Carnival flower girls, *c.* 1908. The girls are lined up with their collecting boxes outside the old pavilion in Victoria Recreation Ground. At this time the carnival was raising money for Taunton Hospital. It had been reintroduced in 1891 and continued nearly every year until the First World War. Revived again in 1922, the carnival continued until 1929 but did not return on a regular basis until 1966. Victoria Recreation Ground was Taunton's first public park opening in 1892.

5

Pubs & Hotels

The Harp Inn, *c.* 1910. The licensee at this time was Henry Emberson. He had lately taken over the pub from John Vickery who ran the business with his daughter Ellen. In 1901 three lodgers staying in the pub were described as 'Timber Throwers'. The wall advertises Charlton Beers from the brewery of Shepton Mallet and the notice on the extreme right refers to the 'Custard Girl'. An MOT station now stands on the site.

Above: Victoria Inn, East Reach, *c.* 1905. Since this time the pub has been completely rebuilt and extended to include the former cottage next door. George Lang from North Newton held the pub in 1901 with his wife Rosina. George retired in his mid-seventies and passed the business to his son William Charles Lang, who was licensee when this photograph was taken. A large crowd of children has appeared to be included in the view.

Ring of Bells, St James Street, *c.* 1940. Like many other pubs in the town the Ring of Bells was completely rebuilt in the 1890s. This view shows the tower of St James's Church, itself rebuilt in 1871–3. On the left are James Street swimming baths which opened in 1929. A few years ago the pub suffered a serious fire and had to be completely refurbished.

The Lethbridge Arms, Bishops Lydeard, *c.* 1905. In 1902 the pub still went under the name Gore Inn; it dated back at least to 1811 when it was used as a stopping point for the Dunster and Minehead Royal Mail coach. In about 1905 the name changed to Lethbridge Arms, referring to the Lethbridge family at Sandhill. The fives court wall built by Sir Thomas Lethbridge can still be seen in the pub car park. The licensee in 1902 was J.E. Heydon.

The Old Inn, Bishops Hull, *c.* 1904. The cart in the distance is standing outside Edwin Baker's bakery shop. This shop and the cottages in the centre of the view were demolished in about 1912 and redeveloped to include a new shop. Next to the pub is a drapery and grocer's shop belonging to W. Rudd. Members of the Knowles family ran the pub up until the First World War. The premises have now been extended to include the shop, although its original outline can still be seen in the brickwork.

The White Horse Inn, Bradford on Tone, *c.* 1905. The publican at this time was J. Berry and the pub was the only one in the parish. The photographer was H. Abraham, stationer of 11 Fore Street, who published many local photographic postcards in the early 1900s.

Ruishton Inn, *c.* 1920. Kenneth Witcombe, the licensee, is sitting proudly in his newly acquired second-hand Ford car.

The Crown Inn, Staplehay, *c.* 1905. In the far distance is Rose Cottage (featured on page 78). The cottage behind the piece of topiary is Billy Bicknell's workshop and house. He was a joiner and coffin maker and lived here with his wife Jessie and daughter Gladys. This area is now the site of a garage. Census records show us that John and Rosina Vincent ran the pub in 1901 and up to the First World War.

The Crown Inn, *c.* 1920. This view would appear to have been taken during James Bowerman's tenancy of the pub in the 1920s. James was preceded by George Bowerman, presumably his father, who held this pub in 1919. Although quite close to Trull, Staplehay is actually part of Pitminster parish.

The Angel Commercial Inn, North Curry, *c*. 1906. The inn's origins were as an alehouse in 1736. Until the coming of the railways it served as a posting inn for stage coaches. Also shown are the premises at 6 Stoke Road that were bought by the tenant Charles Gillard in 1888. From here Mr Gillard ran a saddlers and harness-making business; at this time he was also selling bicycles. The cart bears the letters W.J.T. North Curry and possibly belonged to Walter Temlett.

The same view, *c*. 1960. The Angel Inn closed in 1985. Gillard's shopfront is still in evidence. The Gillard family were running an ironmonger business at Queen Square by the 1930s.

The Bird in Hand, North Curry, *c.* 1960. The chimney of Trevarrick House is in the distance. The pub building was originally thatched but was heightened and re-roofed in about 1900. The sedate pub sign has now been replaced by a picture of a bird of prey.

The Wheelwrights Arms, Stoney Head, just west of Wrantage, *c.* 1930. The pub, now a private house, existed as early as 1813. Originally there may have been a wheelwright's business here. Originally the village had two other pubs. One, the Wrantage Inn, was on the east side of the village, and the other, the Canal Inn, near the centre. Only the Canal Inn remains as a pub.

Rose and Crown Hotel, Lyng, *c.* 1930. This view, looking towards Taunton, was published by Whitby, Light and Lane of Bridgwater.

Rose and Crown, Lyng, *c.* 1940. Notice the cattle in the road. Starkey, Knight and Ford's trademark flying horse can be seen on the wall. Along with Arnold and Hancock the company was one of the area's largest brewers between the wars. The Taunton business started in 1881 when Thomas Starkey bought the Taunton Brewery (now Goodlands Gardens). In 1887 Knight of Bridgwater joined the firm and it traded as Starkey, Knight and Co until 1895. In March that year the business of Ford and Sons of Tiverton was acquired to become Starkey, Knight and Ford. The Taunton Brewery was demolished in the 1960s.

The Farmer's Arms, Combe Florey, *c.* 1930. The parish of Combe Florey had two public houses in 1900 although neither was in the village. The Stag's Head was on the main Minehead road at Seven Ash and the Farmer's Arms close to the railway just north of the village. The pub was rebuilt after a serious fire some years ago and is still open.

Gardener's Arms, Howleigh, *c.* 1910. Howleigh hamlet is in the parish of Pitminster between Blagdon and Lowton. In 1910 the hamlet consisted of a few farms, a parsonage and Howleigh House and Villa. The Gardener's Arms is shown on the Ordnance Survey map of 1891 and directories list a succession of beer retailers up to the 1920s. Today the premises have been completely renovated and are called Hillcrest and Hillcrest Cottage. Part of the long wall has been removed to form a parking space.

Full Moon, South Street, *c.* 1920. This is one of the most recent of Taunton's pubs to be demolished. Like the nearby Forester's Arms the site has been used for residential development. The gentleman in the photograph is Mr Poole, the landlord. Starkey, Knight and Ford owned the pub. In 1902 there were eighty-two public houses in Taunton. Fifty years later this had declined to fifty-two and by the 1970s only forty-five were left. There was also a Full Moon in High Street, two New Inns, two Old Inns and two Somerset Inns.

Opposite, top: Cross Keys Inn, *c.* 1950. The pub is shown on the 1889 Ordnance Survey map although it is likely that it had been rebuilt since then.

Opposite, bottom: The Blackbird Inn, *c.* 1950. The pub dates back to 1773. Originally the pub itself was much smaller with two adjoining cottages, stables and a hayloft. The inn sign was made in about 1938 by the artist Rachel Reckitt (1908–95), who first exhibited at the Society of Wood Engravers in 1933 while a student of Ian Macnab at the Grosvenor School of Modern Art. In 1999 the sign was Grade II listed. One side shows the blackbird's nest with eggs, the other side with chicks. It is constructed of sheet metal, pipes, wire and wood.

The Compass Inn from the end of Trull Road with Cann Street on the right, *c.* 1905. We can see here how narrow this street was at the time. In about 1768 the pub was known as the Square and Compasses. Hanbury and Cotching held it in 1905. The company dated back to 1870, when it traded as G.E. Oram at Mary Street Brewery. In about 1880 a Mr Inglefield bought the business and entered into partnership with Mr Hanbury. New premises were acquired in Canon Street in 1882 and the company became known as Hanbury and Co. until 1894 when there was a change of name to Hanbury and Cotching. Starkey, Knight and Ford bought the business in 1923 and ran the pub under the name Compass Hotel until its demolition in about 1963.

Opposite, top: The George Hotel, *c.* 1965. The hotel probably dated back to the early seventeenth century. Luckily the redevelopments of some thirty-five years ago left the façade intact, although much of the interior was rebuilt. The nearby Old Devon and Somerset Stores, formerly the White Hart, was completely demolished in 1968. The building now houses County Casuals.

Opposite, bottom: The Naval and Military Inn, *c.* 1903. The pub still exists in East Reach although it is not looking quite as smart as it did a hundred years ago. In 1903 the street had four pubs on the north side and nine on the south side. Those no longer existing include the Shakespeare, Wagon and Horses, Rising Sun, Taunton Arms, Seven Stars and, most recently demolished, the Foresters. During the 1880s the large building next to the Naval and Military housed the Servants' Training Home where orphan and destitute girls were trained for domestic service.

The Oak and Acorn and Cherry Grove, *c.* 1910. The pubs co-existed for nearly a hundred years. This photograph was taken from the tramway passing loop between St Andrews Road and Greenway Road. F. Wescombe was the licensee of the Cherry Grove and Mrs Manley ran the Oak and Acorn. Next to the Cherry Grove is Mrs Medicott's grocery shop. The Oak and Acorn closed in recent years but the Cherry Grove underwent refurbishment to emerge as the Grove.

Opposite, top: Clarkes Hotel, 1917. In the foreground are the sheep pens of the livestock market. The builder Mr R.G. Spiller bought the hotel in 1924 and ran it until his death in 1955. He built the third storey in the 1920s and a fourth was added in 1965. When Burton's opened in about 1930 Mr Spiller acquired their top storey and made it into four letting rooms and a flat. He was also responsible for a new portcullis under Castle Bow. The name was changed to Castle Hotel in about 1929.

Opposite, bottom: Cottage Inn, Monkton Heathfield, *c.* 1910. Jasper Woodhouse Leach was the landlord of the pub at this time and continued in occupation until at least 1927. The lady in the doorway is probably Jasper's wife Rhoda. Jasper Leach also had an occupation as carpenter and joiner as did several others of the Leach family in the area. The cottage adjacent to the inn was demolished after 1966. *(Merry Monk Inn)*

The Prince Albert, *c.* 1906. The premises were at 19 Mary Street, formerly the Bird in Hand. This change of name took place in about 1905. The building next to this bears the sign 'Gymnasium' and was part of the Young Women's Christian Association (YWCA) Institute and house. On the right a sign advertises the business of a builder and funeral director, possibly Frederick Gibbs. Mary Street was very narrow until work to complete the inner bypass was undertaken between 1959 and 1965. Selwoods Antiques, formerly on the other side of the street, acquired the premises in about 1960.

6

Religion & Education

Wilton Church and Fons George House, *c.* 1880. The church of St George dates back to the fifteenth century although little of the original building remains. In about 1830 the nave and aisles were enlarged and some twenty years later the tower was demolished and rebuilt. Around this time the churchyard was enlarged to the north and east. It was again enlarged northward in 1884. A vestry was built in 1885 and a reredos added to the chancel in 1887. The photograph was taken before the construction of the lych-gate and before the growth of the beech trees which now obscure Fons George House.

Beehive School, 1948. The school was founded in about 1938 and moved into Henley Lodge on the Wellington Road in 1947. It closed in about 1999.

Beehive school sports, 1948. This photograph shows the rear of the school. Both photographs come from a scrapbook of pupils and staff at the school from 1937 to 1955. Should anyone be interested in viewing further photographs please contact the author.

All Saints' Church, Bathpool, *c.* 1905. The building was erected in 1897 through the efforts of the Revd W. Kinglake and his nephew the Revd F.C. Kinglake. In 1900 the Revd F.C. Kinglake died and a chancel in his honour was added in 1901. The church was not consecrated for weddings or burials; these took place at West Monkton. Behind the church can be seen the Iron Room (featured on page 80). The church closed in 1981 and is now a private house.

Lyng Church and village, *c.* 1905. Here we see the fine church tower of St Bartholomew. The church consists of a chancel, nave and north and south porches. The latter is used as a vestry. Much restoration was done in about 1900 at which time the clock was refurbished with new works and a new dial. The oldest bell dates to 1609.

Above: Building Fivehead Baptist Church, 1904. The foundation stone was laid on 29 September 1904. In this view the workers are taking a well-earned rest. The publisher of this and at least another six postcards appears to be the vicar. One card states 'another of the celebrated "Our Village" series', with the vicarage given as the publisher's address. Profits from the postcards went towards the church tower restoration fund (see below).

Fivehead Church, *c.* 1909. This view shows the tower during the restoration. A service to commemorate the completion of the restoration was held in May 1910. According to directories a new vicarage house was also built in 1905.

Wrantage School, *c.* 1910. The school was built to accommodate fifty children in 1879. Money for its construction was raised by public subscription. After 1900 it was run as a parochial mixed school operating in tandem with North Curry School. The attendance rose to eighty but in 1929 the over elevens were transferred to North Curry. In the early 1940s the school was damaged by a stray parachute mine and it closed shortly after.

North Curry School, *c.* 1906. The school opened in 1848 with a single classroom. By 1870 the premises had grown and accommodated 150 pupils and thirty-three infants. At the time of the photograph this had increased to 190 and this led to a further enlargement of the building in 1911. After this date attendance declined somewhat and the property was beginning to show its age. This resulted in a new school being built at Greenway in 1987.

Bishops Lydeard School, *c.* 1906. The writer of the postcard has identified Ella bottom right and Tom seen shading his eyes. The school building was used for the first time on 20 December 1872. In 1953 the senior children were transferred to Kingsmead School, Wiveliscombe. Bishops Lydeard School remaining solely for primary children.

Bagborough post office and school, *c.* 1905. The building housed both school and post office. Edwin Wale, born in South Petherton in 1844, managed to combine the jobs of sub-postmaster and headmaster. His wife Ella helped in the school together with Edwin's two nieces, Alice and Effie Perry. The schoolhouse had been rebuilt in 1896 for 120 children, although the Wales had only to cope with an average of sixty-two. West Bagborough had a population of 353 in 1901.

Cheddon Fitzpaine School, *c.* 1905. The school was built in 1813 for eighty children. In 1905 Miss R. Pitson was mistress; she had an average attendance of sixty-three children. The village population in 1901 was 271.

Cheddon Fitzpaine schoolchildren, *c.* 1907. Two names are known; Gertrude Priddle in the back row, far right, and her brother Ivan (born 1898) in the middle row, third from left.

Askwith School, *c*. 1914. At the time this was a school for 260 boys. The school was named after William Henry Askwith, Archdeacon of Taunton and vicar of St Mary's Church. He died on 9 April 1911 aged sixty-seven. I am is well acquainted with this view having been a pupil at the school in the early 1960s. There were four classrooms around the hall at this time including Miss Pipe's music room, seen far left, Mr Hughe's English room, and Miss Brown's history room. The headmaster was Mr Mosedale.

Bishop Foxes School, the kindergarten, *c*. 1910. Originally in the Crescent the school moved to new premises at Staplegrove Road in 1904. After enlargement in 1907 the school had six classrooms, a cookery lecture room and kitchen, an art room, chemistry laboratory and a lecture room. The grounds contained model gardens, lawn, tennis and baseball courts and playing fields. The school moved to Kingston Road in 1940 and in later years the building was used as a branch of the Somerset College of Arts and Technology. Recently a serious fire damaged the structure and the building remains empty.

The Convent, *c.* 1904. A series of ten postcards of the convent were sold at the school from about 1904 to 1916. This view of the building is taken from the field at the rear. The card was sent by Kathleen Munster who was a pupil from 1907 to 1912. The property was built as a hospital 'for the relief of the sick poor'. The foundation stone was laid on 29 September 1772.

The Convent, Nuns Field, *c.* 1904. Although built as a hospital the building never fulfilled that role, becoming a private house in 1793. The third order of St Francis acquired the house in about 1807 and built a large new wing between 1808 and 1812, also adding a chapel in 1811. Cloisters were built in 1859 and a new farmhouse added in 1868. After many extensions and modernisation St Joseph's Convent closed in 1978 and until recently was used by Kings College. The extensive grounds have now been used for a housing development.

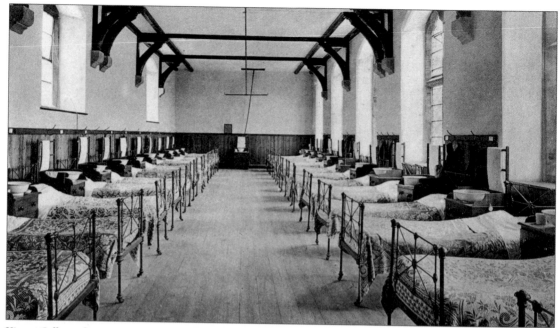

Kings College dormitory, c. 1908. The series of postcards published by P.A. Buchanan and Co. give an interesting insight into school life in the early 1900s. This dormitory at Kings College appears very spartan and cold. Every iron bed is identical and so are the washing facilities beside each bed. The buildings at South Road were erected in 1870 in 15 acres of ground formerly part of the old Taunton racecourse.

Taunton Girls' School, c. 1925. The school opened in Park Street in 1922 but within a few months had moved into St Mary's vicarage. The school had forty-six girls and seven boys of kindergarten age. The school was known informally as 'Mrs Rapp's', after the principal. A former pupil described it as an 'old fashioned school of the private kind'. The girls were sent there to become 'little ladies'. At the end of 1927 Mrs Rapp moved back to Park Street, and the school was relocated to Burnham-on-Sea by 1930.

7

Villages

Isle Abbots post office and shop, *c.* 1904. The ladies in the doorway are Anna and Ellen Patten, the two unmarried sisters who ran the business. The eldest, Anna, was born in the village in 1835. The population of the village was only 265 but early postcards hint at a busy social scene with views of sports days and social occasions.

Lowton post office, *c*. 1908. This postcard is taken from the same set as the Gardener's Arms on page 101. The Mappledoram family ran the post office and shop for over forty years. At this time William was the sub-postmaster, a position he combined with that of agricultural labourer. He was assisted by his wife Jane, daughter Mary and grandson William Cook. In the 1920s William's wife Jane ran the business but in 1935 a Mrs Mary Ann Mappledoram was in charge. The last shopkeeper was Mrs Bobbet whose daughter Susan went to Trull School.

Fivehead post office, *c*. 1904. This rural post office was one of the first to receive its letters via Taunton. Sub-postmistress Mary Rosina Milton received her daily batch at 4.30 a.m. These were sorted and sent out for local delivery before 7.30 a.m. The population of the village in 1901 was 413. It had a wall letter-box for posting close to the Baptist Chapel. The postcard is one of the 'Our Village' series produced to raise funds for the church tower restoration.

Curland post office and shop, *c.* 1910. This was situated at the crossroads at Stoneleigh. The post office also served the large parish of Staple Fitzpaine which only had a wall box. In 1901 Curland's population was 135 with 257 people at Staple. The Curland children went to school at Staple. Samuel Rowsell was sub-postmaster at Curland at this time.

The Stores, Bagborough, *c.* 1906. This is typical of the village shops at the time. Frederick William Sealey, seen standing by his horse, was both a baker and grocer. This business had started in the early 1890s.

North Curry, c. 1906. This view shows children standing along the wall in front of the Old Brewery building. At this time there was a malthouse here, owned by James Temlett. His son Walter ran the business from about 1910 to the 1920s. People have climbed the gas lamp at the junction to Church Road. This was removed when the First World War memorial was erected.

Opposite, top: Amphlett's Kingston Stores, c. 1909. Alexander Amphlett only had the stores for a few years around 1910. The 1901 Census places him in Chelsea at that time aged thirty-four and serving as a grocer's assistant. This postcard was sent to a client in an attempt to offload some cheap butter as the store was overstocked.

Opposite, bottom: Victorian Jubilee Monument, North Curry, c. 1906. The monument was built at the cost of £250, the money raised by local subscription and an outdoor fête. The foundation stone was laid by twelve-year-old Dorothy Barrett of Moredon on 26 July 1897. The lady in this view stands outside James Bradbury's bakery and sweet shop.

Bathpool, *c.* 1905. This is a view of the main road taken from the approach to the railway bridge. The long building in the centre to the left is the Congregational chapel.

The Bridge Stores, Bathpool, *c.* 1922. The sign on the wall states 'J. Abbot Steam Bakery and Post Office'. Mr Abbot appears to have been a short term tenant of the property as directories list Joseph Lockyer from 1923 to 1935.

George H. Tytherleigh's Stores, Hatch Beauchamp, *c.* 1905. Mr Tytherleigh stands in the doorway with one of his several daughters who later travelled by train to Taunton to attend Bishop Fox's school. By the 1930s the village post office had occupied this site and the thatched cottage in the distance had been reconstructed to include a tiled roof.

Comeytrowe Lane, *c.* 1917. This view has hardly changed although tall trees are little in evidence today. The first block of houses was demolished some years ago and a pair of modern properties built on the site. The last block in the row is called Jubilee Terrace, with the date 1897.

Stoke St Gregory, *c.* 1905. The children are standing in Well Lane. Partially obscured by the Royal Oak public house, the church of St Gregory had been restored in the 1880s and a clock was added in 1897 to celebrate Queen Victoria's Diamond Jubilee. The school on the right was built in 1857 on land given by the Revd R.W. Moor. It was run at this time by Ernest and Annie Pullen and had an average attendance of 148. The village population in 1901 was 1331.

Bathpool, *c.* 1914. The view shows J. Trott's general store at the corner of the Swingbridge Road. The large building on the left is Acacia House in whose grounds the modern estate Acacia Gardens was built.

Wrantage, c. 1910. The village had a population of 302 in 1901 but this has since declined to about 200. The school, Methodist chapel, post office and two public houses have closed over the years. In the centre of the village are the remains of the Chard Canal, which was opened in 1842 and closed 1866. From the village an inclined plane took the canal to the mile long tunnel through Crimson Hill.

Curload, c. 1905. Photographers often captioned their cards 'Carload' or 'Curry Load'. The building on the right is Curry Load Farm.

ACKNOWLEDGEMENTS

This is my fifth book for Sutton Publishing and the first since *Taunton – The Changing Face of the Town and its People*, published in 2000. Since then my collection of old photographs has continued to grow and it has been a pleasure to produce this new compilation. Most of my photographs come from my own endeavours but the following people have lent items for copying or helped with research.

Philip Perryman, Pete Rose, Marion Gould, Mrs Arberry, Steve Pike, Phylis Smale, Mrs Iris Williams, John Upham, Tony Norris, Graham Crean, Rosemary Durie, the Merry Monk Inn, Doug Kent and Brian Bunney. Many thanks also to go to Vicky Breeze for typing and proofreading.

If readers have further information or photographs I could copy, please contact me at 36 Scafell Close, Taunton, Somerset, TA1 4LG.

Staple Fitzpaine Cricket Club members in fancy dress, *c.* 1903.